For my brother Steve
and my sister Julie.

Follow and Do
Holy Baptism

Written and Illustrated by **Joni Walker**

CONCORDIA PUBLISHING HOUSE · SAINT LOUIS

Dear Parents,

When we see our babies for the first time, it's almost impossible to comprehend the concept of **ORIGINAL SIN** in them. Yet it's there. Babies seem to be completely innocent; nevertheless, they are guilty of sin that separates them from a loving God.

Once and for all, Jesus overcame that separation. He went to the cross and took upon Himself the punishment for sin, original and otherwise. Now we can freely and confidently confess that we believe in one Baptism for the remission of sins and in life everlasting. As St. Paul said in Romans 6:3–5, "all of us who were baptized into Christ Jesus were baptized into His death … in order that, just as Christ was raised from the dead through the glory of the Father, we too may live a new life … united with Him in His resurrection."

From the moment we know about them, even in the months before they are born, we joyfully do all we can to care for our children so they grow physically and emotionally into healthy, happy people.

A developing child also needs other loving adults. Parents, grandparents, aunts, uncles, siblings, friends, and caregivers individually and collectively contribute to the development of our children. Among those people are the Godparents we choose, people like us who are dedicated to bringing up our child in the nurture and admonition of the Word of God.

It is our parental responsibility to bring our child forward to be baptized. God commands it. It is also our great joy because Baptism is not about what *we* do—it is about what God does. It is through the washing and renewal of water and Word that our child's sins are forgiven and faith is created, once and for all.

Beyond our own parenting efforts, our love and care are surpassed only by that given by God in His Word and Sacraments. Although we are sinners, we are saints as well, made righteous through the work of Christ. Thanks be to God!

First
What is Baptism?

Baptism is not just plain water, but it is the water included in God's command and combined with God's word.

My baby brother is going to be baptized today.

5

WHICH IS THAT WORD OF GOD?

Christ our Lord says in the last chapter of Matthew:
> "Therefore go and make disciples of all nations,
> baptizing them in the name of the Father and of
> the Son and of the Holy Spirit" (Matthew 28:19).

Would you like to come to Vacation Bible School with us?

7

SECOND
WHAT BENEFITS DOES BAPTISM GIVE?

It works forgiveness of sins, rescues from death and the devil,
and gives eternal salvation to all who believe this,
as the words and promises of God declare.

I am not afraid of the devil because God protects me.

WHICH ARE THESE WORDS AND PROMISES OF GOD?

Christ our Lord says in the last chapter of Mark:
   "Whoever believes and is baptized will be saved, but
   whoever does not believe will be condemned" (Mark 16:16).

I will always believe in God.

Third
How can water do such great things?

Certainly not just water, but the word of God in and with the water does these things, along with the faith which trusts this word of God in the water.

When someone is baptized the water is special because it is combined with God's Word.

13

For without God's word the water is plain water and no Baptism.
But with the word of God it is a Baptism, that is, a life-giving water,
rich in grace, and a washing of the new birth in the Holy Spirit,
as St. Paul says in Titus, chapter three.

I am happy
that my brother
is God's child,
like me.

15

"He saved us through the washing of rebirth and renewal by the Holy Spirit, whom He poured out on us generously through Jesus Christ our Savior, so that, having been justified by His grace, we might become heirs having the hope of eternal life. This is a trustworthy saying" (Titus 3:5–8).

I know that
Jesus died for me.

FOURTH

WHAT DOES SUCH BAPTIZING WITH WATER INDICATE?

It indicates that the Old Adam in us should
by daily contrition and repentance be drowned
and die with all sins and evil desires,

Dear God,
Forgive me for the
bad things I said
and did today.

19

and that a new man should daily emerge and arise
to live before God in righteousness and purity forever.

Thank you God,
for this new day.

21

WHERE IS THIS WRITTEN?

St. Paul writes in Romans chapter six: "We were therefore buried with Him through baptism into death in order that, just as Christ was raised from the dead through the glory of the Father, we too may live a new life" (Romans 6:4).

I am glad I was baptized. Someday, I will live in heaven with Jesus.

23

Published by Concordia Publishing House
3558 S. Jefferson Avenue, St. Louis, MO 63118-3968
1-800-325-3040 • www.cph.org

1   2   3   4   5   6   7   8   9   10   14   13   12   11   10   09   08   07   06   05